Abraham Lincoln

Jane A. Schott

LERNER PUBLICATIONS COMPANY • MINNEAPOLIS

Map on p. 25 by Laura Westlund
Illustrations by Tim Parlin

Text copyright © 2002 by Jane A. Schott
Illustrations copyright © 2002 by Lerner Publications Company
Reprinted in 2006

All rights reserved. International copyright secured. No part of this book may be
reproduced, stored in a retrieval system, or transmitted in any form or by any
means—electronic, mechanical, photocopying, recording, or otherwise—without
the prior written permission of Lerner Publishing Group, except for the inclusion
of brief quotations in an acknowledged review.

Lerner Publications Company
A division of Lerner Publishing Group
241 First Avenue North
Minneapolis, MN 55401 U.S.A.

Website address: www.lernerbooks.com

Library of Congress Cataloging-in-Publication Data

Schott, Jane A.
    Abraham Lincoln / by Jane A. Schott.
        p.   cm. — (History maker bios)
    Includes bibliographical references and index.
    ISBN-13: 978–0–8225–0196–1 (lib. bdg. : alk. paper)
    ISBN-10: 0–8225–0196–1 (lib. bdg. : alk. paper)
        1. Lincoln, Abraham, 1809–1865—Juvenile literature.
    2. Presidents—United States—Biography—Juvenile literature.
    [1. Lincoln, Abraham, 1809–1865. 2. Presidents.] I. Title. II. Series.
    E457.905.S36 2002
    973.7'092—dc21   2001003273

Manufactured in the United States of America
2 3 4 5 6 7 – JR – 11 10 09 08 07 06

TABLE OF CONTENTS

INTRODUCTION

Abraham Lincoln was president of the United States from 1861 to 1865. While he was president, there was a war between Southern states and Northern states over slavery. Lincoln was against slavery. He thought all people should be free. The war was long and hard, but Lincoln never gave up. At the end of the war, North and South became one country again. Soon after that, all slaves were free.

Many people think Abraham Lincoln was the greatest president our country has had.

This is his story.

1 GROWING UP

On February 12, 1809, a cold winter wind blew through the bare trees near Hodgenville, Kentucky. Smoke rose from the chimney of a little log cabin. Thomas Lincoln had built a big fire in the fireplace to keep the cabin warm. A baby was about to be born.

Suddenly, a tiny cry was heard. Nancy Lincoln held her new son in her arms. His name was Abraham Lincoln.

Abraham, his mother, father, and si
Sarah lived in the little cabin until Abr
was two years old. Then they moved.
Thomas Lincoln wanted farmland where he
could grow a better crop of corn. He found it
near a place called Knob Creek, Kentucky.

At Knob Creek, young Abraham helped
his father plant corn and pumpkins. He
played in the woods. He caught sunfish in
the creek. For a little while, he went to
school with other children who lived
nearby. But often there was no teacher.
Then there was no school for the children.

The one-room log cabin where Abraham was born was rebuilt in 1917.

Abraham's father,
Thomas Lincoln

Some people said that Thomas Lincoln was not really the owner of the Knob Creek farm. Thomas was afraid his land would be taken from him. Also, many farmers in Kentucky owned slaves. Thomas thought slavery was wrong, and he did not want his family to live where slavery was practiced.

When Abraham was seven years old, Thomas moved the family to Indiana. The land in Indiana was covered with forest. Trees, vines, and bushes grew so close together that Thomas had to cut a path for his family to walk to their new home.

In Indiana, Abraham learned how to swing an ax. He helped his father build a new log cabin and clear land to plant corn. Chopping down trees, hauling away logs, and burning out stumps was hard work for a young boy. But Abraham soon got used to it. It took many weeks to clear a field for farming. It would take years to clear the whole farm.

Abraham spent time with his mother, too. Nancy Lincoln could not read. But she wanted Abraham and Sarah to go to school and learn to read. In the evenings, she told her children Bible stories. Sarah and Abraham loved to listen.

Nancy Lincoln watches as Abraham chops wood.

When Abraham was nine, his mother died from a disease called "milk sickness." Abraham and Sarah were filled with terrible sadness. Abraham worked harder at chopping trees and clearing the land. He didn't want to think about his mother being gone. But even the hard work could not make him forget the awful loneliness of not having his mother.

SKINNY BUT STRONG

When he was fifteen, Abraham was almost six feet tall. He was very thin, but people were surprised at how strong he was. Once he picked up a six-hundred-pound chicken coop and moved it by himself. He also had a reputation as the best wrestler in his county—maybe even the entire state. No one who wrestled against Abraham could bring him down.

Sarah Bush Johnston became Abraham's stepmother in December 1819. Abraham and "Sally," as she was known, became very close.

Thomas Lincoln went back to Kentucky to find a new wife and mother for his children. He married Sarah Bush Johnston. Her husband had died. She needed a home for herself and her three children.

Sarah Bush Johnston was a kind woman. Abraham and Sarah soon loved her. She wanted all of the children to go to school. Abraham knew his mother had wanted him to learn to read and write, and he liked learning. On the days that he didn't have to work with his father, Abraham walked the two miles to school.

A page from Abraham's workbook

The school was called a "blab school" because the children repeated all of their lessons aloud. Although Abraham went to school only a few days at a time, he learned what he could. Then he read and studied at home. Children at the school started calling him "Abe." He didn't like the nickname, but he got used to it.

All of the studying made Abe a good reader and writer. Many of the Lincolns' neighbors could not write, and sometimes people would ask Abe to write letters for them.

Abe loved reading and writing more than anything else. Even though he was tired from working all day, he would spend the evening reading by the light of the fire. Sometimes he would walk miles just to borrow a book.

Abe grew into a very tall young man. His clothes were never long enough. His ankles showed below his pants, and his wrists stuck out of his sleeves. He was thin, too, but all the hard work on the farm had made his muscles strong. Soon he was ready to leave home and see the world.

Abe said that his best friend was any person who got him a book he hadn't read.

2 HONEST ABE

The summer that Abe was nineteen, he got a job taking a flatboat of supplies down the Mississippi River to New Orleans. A flatboat was a big raft that was moved along by the current of the river. Sometimes it got stuck and Abe had to push it along with a pole. Day after day, Abe watched the muddy Mississippi roll by as the flatboat drifted farther south. He had never been so far from home.

Many white people in the Southern states owned slaves. While he was on his trip, Abe saw slaves working in cotton fields. He saw a place where slaves were bought and sold. He kept thinking about how wrong slavery was. One person should not be allowed to buy another person. No person should be forced to work for another without being paid.

When the journey was over, Abe returned home. But he never forgot what he had seen.

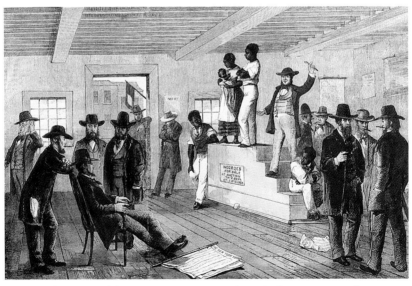

Slaves being sold at auction. By the early 1800s, about a third of the people living in the South were slaves.

When Abe was twenty-one, in 1830, his family moved to Illinois. They left Indiana late in the winter. Ice and mud made the trails dangerous for the covered wagon pulled by oxen. But at last they reached their new home. Once again, Abe helped his father chop down trees and clear land.

Abe was eager to move out of his family's house and live on his own. In July of 1831, he moved to New Salem, another town in Illinois. He got jobs chopping wood and working with the blacksmith.

Abe said about his ax that he "was almost constantly handling that most useful instrument."

Black Hawk was a Sauk Indian chief. He fought against white settlers who were taking Indian land.

In the spring of 1832, Abe signed up to be a soldier in the Black Hawk War. This was a fight between settlers and Indians over land in the area. The men in Abe's company elected him as captain. They liked that he was strong, honest, and a good storyteller. The war only lasted a few months, and Abe never had to fight.

Back in New Salem, Abe borrowed money and bought a store with another man. But the other man died, and the store went out of business. Abe knew he would have to work many years to pay back the money he had borrowed.

Abe owned this general store with his partner, William Berry.

As he worked in New Salem, Abe had many ideas about how to make the state of Illinois better. Abe thought he would like to be a lawmaker in the Illinois state government. He ran for a position in the state legislature, but he didn't win.

Abe worked at several different jobs. None of the jobs seemed right for him, and he didn't make much money. But he knew he had to pay off the debt. People began to call him "Honest Abe" because he worked so long and hard to repay the money he owed.

In 1834, Abe ran for the legislature again. This time, he won. To prepare for his new job, Abe bought the first suit he had ever owned.

Abe moved to Vandalia, the capital of Illinois. He attended the law-making meetings of the state government. At first, Abe just listened to other lawmakers talk about their ideas for new laws. After a while, he began to talk, too.

Joshua Fry Speed was Abe's best friend while he lived in Illinois. The two even shared a room for a while.

The first known photograph of Abe, taken in the 1840s

Abe had grown up poor, so he always wanted to help make people's lives better. He thought the state should spend money to build roads and railroads and to make the rivers easier for boats to travel. Like his stories, his ideas were good and other people listened.

Abe knew he would be a better lawmaker if he knew more about the laws. He decided to become a lawyer. He borrowed law books from his friends and studied hard, just like he had when he was younger. After three years, he took a test to become a lawyer and passed.

Abe was excited about his success. Being a lawyer would make him a better lawmaker. It would also earn him a better living.

One night, Abe went to a party at the home of some friends. There he met a pretty young woman with bright blue eyes and soft brown hair. Her name was Mary Todd. After that evening, Abe and Mary saw each other often. Three years later, on November 4, 1842, they were married. Soon their son Robert Todd was born. Two and a half years later, another son, Edward, was born.

IN LOVE WITH A BLOCKHEAD

It was lucky that Abe and Mary Todd fell in love at all. A couple of years before they met, Abe had asked another woman to marry him. She said no. Abe's feelings were hurt, and he decided never to marry anyone. He said he wasn't good enough to marry, and anyone who loved him must be a "blockhead." But when he met the beautiful and smart Mary Todd three years later, he changed his mind right away.

Mary Todd Lincoln called Abe "the kindest man, most tender husband, and loving father in the world."

Abe worked as a lawyer in Springfield, Illinois. Often he "traveled the circuit." He rode his horse to small towns to help people with their legal problems. When Abe returned home, his children would rush out to meet him.

3 ARGUING OVER SLAVERY

In 1846, Abe was elected to the House of Representatives, a group of lawmakers for the whole United States. He and Mary moved to Washington, D.C. At first, Mary enjoyed living in the nation's capital, but Abe was hardly ever home. Mary became lonely. She and the little boys went to stay with her father in Kentucky.

When Abe's term in the House of Representatives ended, in 1849, he went back to being a full-time lawyer.

Abe had little time to think about his family. Every day was full of meetings. The representatives often talked about slavery. Some thought all slaves should be freed. Others thought people who owned slaves should be allowed to keep them.

At that time, the law said that only people in states south of Missouri could own slaves. But the country was growing. New states were joining the United States, and some people wanted slavery to be allowed in the new states.

Stephen Douglas, a senator from Illinois, was trying to pass a law called the Kansas-Nebraska Act. This law would allow new states to decide whether they wanted to be "slave" or "free" states.

Abe didn't want to see slavery spread into new states. He spoke out against slavery and the Kansas-Nebraska Act.

The United States in 1854

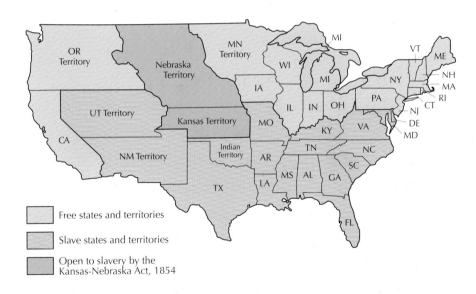

Free states and territories

Slave states and territories

Open to slavery by the
Kansas-Nebraska Act, 1854

Abe wanted to allow slavery only in the states that already had it. He believed slavery would die out if it did not spread to new states.

When Stephen Douglas heard that Abe would be his opponent in the 1858 Senate race, he said, "I shall have my hands full."

Abe knew that more people would listen to him if he were a senator. In 1854, he ran for election as United States senator from Illinois. But he lost the election, and the Kansas-Nebraska Act became a law.

In 1858, Abe again ran for the United States Senate, this time against Stephen Douglas. Abe challenged Douglas to a series of public discussions called debates. Abe wanted people to hear their different ideas, especially on slavery.

The more Abe thought about slavery, the stronger he felt. It wasn't just wrong—it was splitting the United States apart, turning slave states and free states against each other. Abe called the United States "a house divided against itself." He believed that the United States would have to become all free or all slave in order to survive.

EXCITED LISTENERS

Watching the Lincoln-Douglas debates, people thought that Lincoln looked awkward, ugly, and poorly dressed compared to Douglas. But Lincoln showed them that even though he was a clumsy country boy, he was an excellent debater. At the end of one debate, two farmers were so excited by Lincoln's words that they rushed onto the stage and carried Lincoln above them. His long, thin legs dangled from their shoulders.

Thousands of people came to hear the Lincoln-Douglas debates. Douglas tried to convince people that states should be allowed to decide for themselves about slavery. Abe argued that slavery was wrong and should not be allowed to spread to any new states.

Although Abe did well in the debates, Stephen Douglas won the election. Abe was sad because he wanted to fight against slavery as a senator. But he didn't stop making speeches. Abe became a very popular speaker in free states such as Ohio and Indiana.

This drawing of Abe at one of the debates shows what a lively speaker he was.

THE COUNTRY AT WAR

4

In 1860, the nation was getting ready to elect a new president. The Republican Party liked Abraham Lincoln's ideas on slavery and his popular speeches. They asked him to run for president. The Democrats chose two men, Stephen Douglas and John C. Breckinridge.

Everyone in the country knew that a vote for Lincoln would be a vote against slavery. Most people who owned slaves lived in the South. Some Southern states said that if Lincoln was elected, they would secede from the Union. That meant they would no longer be a part of the United States. When the votes were counted, Lincoln had won. All of the free states had voted for him, but not a single slave state had chosen him.

A campaign poster for Lincoln and his vice president Hannibal Hamlin

In his inaugural address, Lincoln told Southerners, "We are not enemies, but friends. We must not be enemies."

Abraham Lincoln became president on March 4, 1861. He knew he faced a job that many people felt was impossible. He had to find a way to keep the United States together. Before he even took office, seven Southern states had already seceded. Four more seceded soon after he took office. The seceded states called themselves the Confederate States of America.

Many Southern families had picnics during the attack on Fort Sumter. They thought the war would be quick, and easily won by the South.

Many people thought only a war could decide whether slavery should be allowed. Already, the Southern states had an army called the Confederate Army. The Civil War began when the Confederate Army fired their guns at Fort Sumter in South Carolina on April 12, 1861.

A new Union Army was quickly formed in the North. Thousands of men came to fight in it. But there were not enough guns, uniforms, or leaders for the soldiers. The Confederate Army easily won many battles.

Lincoln chose new leaders for the Union soldiers. People gave money for guns and uniforms. A new law let freed slaves join the Union Army. Still, the North lost battles. Thousands of men were dying. Lincoln was worried and often could not sleep at night. People noticed the dark circles under his eyes and new lines on his long, thin face.

Only his wife and children gave him happiness during this time. Edward had died in 1850, but Mary had given birth to two more sons, Willie and Tad.

The Lincoln family. LEFT TO RIGHT: Mary, Willie, Robert Todd, Tad, and Abraham Lincoln

Lincoln met with General George McClellan on the battlefield at Antietam, Maryland, in October 1862.

Then in February of 1862, Willie and Tad became ill with high fevers. Tad got well, but Willie died. Mary was so sick with sadness that she stayed in bed for months. Lincoln had to hide his sorrow and keep working to end the war.

Lincoln knew that as long as there was slavery, North and South could not be one nation. In September of 1862, he wrote the Emancipation Proclamation. After January 1, 1863, it would be against the law for anyone in the South to own slaves. This would be the first step toward ending all slavery in the United States.

After three days of heavy fighting in July of 1863, the Union Army won a bloody battle at Gettysburg, Pennsylvania. More than five thousand soldiers died. In November, Lincoln went to Gettysburg to create a national cemetery for the soldiers who had died. In his famous speech called the Gettysburg Address, Lincoln promised that "this nation, under God, shall have a new birth of freedom."

Lincoln gives his famous Gettysburg Address.

The Confederates continued to win many battles for the South. The skillful general Robert E. Lee was in charge of all Confederate forces. Lincoln began to think the North might lose the war. Then, in March of 1864, he chose Ulysses S. Grant as general of the entire Union Army.

Led by Grant, the North attacked the South again and again. Many soldiers were killed and wounded, but Grant would not give up. Lincoln said he was like a bulldog that sank his teeth in and would not let go.

VISITING THE WOUNDED

Lincoln cared about all soldiers in the war, from the North or the South. He visited one dying Confederate soldier and asked to shake his hand. The man agreed, even though Lincoln was a stranger. "There should be no enemies in this place," the soldier said. Then Lincoln told him, "I am Abraham Lincoln, president of the United States," and the soldier allowed Lincoln to hold his hand.

5 THE END OF THE WAR

In the summer of 1864, Lincoln ran for a second term as president. He promised if he won, he would work to pass a law that would end slavery in the United States.

He won easily, and on January 31, 1865, Congress passed the Thirteenth Amendment. After all the states in the country agreed, it would be against the law to own slaves.

In March of 1865, Lincoln gave a speech. His face had more lines and he was very thin, but he spoke with a strong voice. He said that Northerners and Southerners must work together for peace and treat each other well when the war was over. He said the people of the United States should try "to bind up the nation's wounds."

Just a few weeks later, the Civil War was over. On April 9, 1865, General Robert E. Lee surrendered to General Ulysses S. Grant. In Washington, church bells rang, cannons were fired, and people cheered.

This drawing for Lincoln's reelection campaign was titled "Long Abraham a Little Longer."

All the worry and hard decisions of the war had made Lincoln look and feel much older than he was.

Lincoln spoke to a crowd at the White House and told them his plans for peace. He would welcome the Confederate States back into the Union. They would be allowed to keep their own state governments, but they would have to accept the Thirteenth Amendment. All slaves would be free.

Lincoln was tired. He was only fifty-six years old. But all of the worry and hard decisions during the war had worn him down. Almost 620,000 soldiers had died. Even the happiness of having the country reunited could not erase the sadness of families who had lost fathers, brothers, and sons.

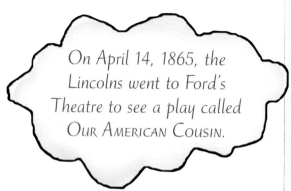

On April 14, 1865, the Lincolns went to Ford's Theatre to see a play called OUR AMERICAN COUSIN.

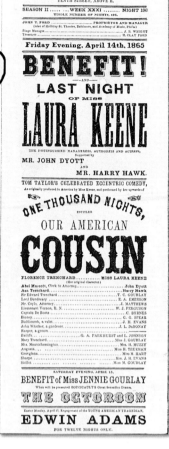

But there were some people who still felt the president was wrong and that they should be allowed to own slaves. Lincoln got many angry letters from people threatening to hurt or kill him, but he ignored them.

On April 14, 1865, Lincoln and Mary went to the theater. Lincoln told his wife he was the happiest he had been in months.

For a little while, they laughed and enjoyed the play. But near the end of the show, an actor named John Wilkes Booth ran up behind the president and shot him. Booth was a Southerner who believed that black people should be slaves, not free. He hated Lincoln for ending slavery.

Lincoln was carried to a house across the street. He was unconscious, and the doctors said he would not live.

John Wilkes Booth was a famous actor from a family of famous actors. Before he killed Lincoln, he wrote in a letter, "This country was formed for the white, not for the black man."

FATHER ABRAHAM

People called Abraham Lincoln Father Abraham because they loved him like a father. When Lincoln was killed, millions of people felt like they had lost their own father. After Lincoln died, even his critics admitted he was a kind and unselfish man.

Mary and their oldest son, Robert Todd, stayed with him through the night. When morning came, the president died. One of Lincoln's secretaries who was there said sadly, "Now he belongs to the ages."

A funeral train carried the president's body back to Illinois. It stopped in cities and towns along the way for special services. The American people said good-bye to Abraham Lincoln. He had accomplished his goal of reuniting the country, but he had paid for it with his life. On May 4, 1865, Abraham Lincoln was buried in Springfield, Illinois, next to his sons Edward and Willie.

Though Lincoln was dead, his dream of freedom for all Americans lived on. He had worked against great odds to free the slaves, and to keep the United States together as one country. Because of his hard work, all Americans are free.

Lincoln's funeral procession in Washington, D.C.

TIMELINE

ABRAHAM LINCOLN
WAS BORN ON
FEBRUARY 12, 1809

In the year . . .

1818 Abraham's mother died from milk sickness. Age 9

1828 he rode a flatboat down the Mississippi and saw a slave auction in New Orleans.

1834 he was elected to the Illinois state legislature. he began to study law.

1842 he married Mary Todd November 4. Age 33

1843 his first child, Robert Todd, was born August 1.

1846 his son Edward was born March 10. he was elected to the U.S. House of Representatives.

1850 his son Edward died. his son William (Willie) was born December 21.

1853 his son Thomas (Tad) was born April 4.

1858 he ran against Stephen Douglas for the U.S. Senate, and they had seven public debates.

1860 he won the United States presidential election. Age 51 South Carolina seceded from the Union.

1861 he was sworn in as president March 4. the South attacked Fort Sumter April 12, starting the Civil War.

1862 his son Willie died February 20.

1863 he signed the Emancipation Proclamation January 1. he gave the Gettysburg Address November 19.

1865 he was sworn in for his second term as president March 4. Congress passed the Thirteenth Amendment. the South surrendered April 9 and the Civil War ended. he was shot by John Wilkes Booth April 14. he died April 15. Age 56

THE LINCOLN MEMORIAL

In the years after Abraham Lincoln's death, many people in the United States wanted to build a memorial to him. On February 12, 1914, workers began to build the Lincoln Memorial in Washington, D.C. It was the 105th anniversary of Lincoln's birth. When the memorial was dedicated on Memorial Day 1922, Robert Todd Lincoln was the guest of honor. Robert Todd was Lincoln's only living son.

The Lincoln Memorial is a beautiful, white marble building about the size of a football field, held up by huge pillars. A nineteen-foot-tall statue of Lincoln sits inside. His two most famous speeches—the Gettysburg Address and his second Inaugural Address—are carved into the walls.

Anyone can visit the Lincoln Memorial. It is open twenty-four hours a day, seven days a week. And it is free.

FURTHER READING

NONFICTION

Haskins, James. *The Day Fort Sumter Was Fired on: A Photo History of the Civil War.* New York: Scholastic, Inc., 1995. Documents the course of the Civil War and its effect on women, blacks, and children.

Murphy, Jim. *The Boy's War: Confederate and Union Soldiers Talk About the Civil War.* New York: Clarion Books, 1990. Diary entries, personal letters, and photographs describe the experiences of boys, sixteen years old and younger, who fought in the Civil War.

Ransom, Candice F. *Children of the Civil War.* Minneapolis: Carolrhoda Books, Inc., 1998. Explores the lives of children during the Civil War, including those who joined armies, others who stayed home, and the large numbers made homeless because of the conflict.

FICTION

Crist-Evans, Craig. *Moon Over Tennessee: A Boy's Civil War Journal.* Boston: Houghton Mifflin, 1999. A thirteen-year-old boy sets off with his father from their farm in Tennessee to join the Confederate forces on their way to fight at Gettysburg. Told in the form of diary entries.

Hansen, Joyce. *Which Way Freedom?* New York: Avon Books, 1992. Obi escapes from slavery during the Civil War, joins a black Union regiment, and soon becomes involved in the bloody fighting at Fort Pillow, Tennessee.

Wisler, G. Clifton. *Mr. Lincoln's Drummer.* New York: Lodestar Books, 1995. Recounts the courageous exploits of an eleven-year-old Civil War drummer who became the youngest recipient of the Congressional Medal of Honor.

WEBSITES

America's Library (Abraham Lincoln page)
www.americaslibrary.gov/cgi-bin/page.cgi/aa/lincoln
An entertaining and educational look at Lincoln. Includes stories, photos, maps, prints, manuscripts, and audio and video recordings from the collections of the Library of Congress.

Lincoln Home National Historic Site
www.nps.gov/liho/index.htm
The National Park Service's site for the home Lincoln owned in Springfield, Illinois. Provides history, as well as a virtual tour of the house.

The White House (Abraham Lincoln page)
www.whitehouse.gov/history/presidents/al16.html
The Abraham Lincoln page of the official website of the White House. Contains a special section for kids.

SELECT BIBLIOGRAPHY

Donald, David Herbert. *Lincoln.* New York: Simon and Schuster, 1995.

Holzer, Harold, ed. *Lincoln As I Knew Him: Gossip, Tributes & Revelations from His Best Friends and Worst Enemies.* Chapel Hill, NC: Algonquin Books, 1999.

Kunhardt, Jr., Philip B., Philip B. Kunhardt III, and Peter W. Kunhardt. *Lincoln: An Illustrated Biography.* New York: Random House, 1999.

Neely, Jr., Mark E. *Last Best Hope of Earth.* Cambridge, MA: Harvard University Press, 1993.

Redway, Maurine Whorton, and Dorothy Kendall Bracken. *Marks of Lincoln on Our Land.* New York: Hastings House Publisher, Inc., 1957.

INDEX

Acknowledgments

For photographs and artwork: © CORBIS, p. 4; Independent Picture Service, pp. 7, 38, 45; Library of Congress, pp. 8, 12, 16, 20, 22, 30, 33, 34, 39, 43; © North Wind Picture Archives, pp. 9, 11, 13, 15, 24, 26, 28, 31, 32, 35, 40; American Antiquarian Society, p. 17; Illinois State Historical Library, pp. 18, 19; National Archives, p. 41. Front cover: © North Wind Picture Archives, (photo); Corbis Royalty Free Images, (frame). Back cover: PhotoDisc Royalty Free by Getty Images.
For quoted material: pp. 16, 27, 31, Roy P. Basler, ed., *The Collected Works of Abraham Lincoln*, vol. 4 (New Brunswick, NJ: Rutgers University Press, 1953–55); p. 22, William Herndon, *Life of Lincoln* (New York: Albert & Charles Boni, 1930); p. 26, John Forney, *Anecdotes of Public Men* (New York: Harper & Brothers, 1881); p. 35, Roy P. Basler, ed., *The Collected Works of Abraham Lincoln*, vol. 7; p. 36, Charles M. Segal, ed., *Conversations with Lincoln* (New York: G. P. Putnam's Sons, 1961); p. 38, Roy P. Basler, ed., *The Collected Works of Abraham Lincoln*, vol. 8; p. 41, John Rhodehamel and Louise Taper, eds., *"Right or Wrong, God Judge Me": the Writings of John Wilkes Booth* (Urbana: University of Illinois Press, 1997).